England Cobden Club , Edward North Buxton

The ABC of Free Trade

England Cobden Club , Edward North Buxton

The ABC of Free Trade

ISBN/EAN: 9783744662451

Printed in Europe, USA, Canada, Australia, Japan

Cover: Foto ©Suzi / pixelio.de

More available books at **www.hansebooks.com**

PRICE THREEPENCE.

THE

ABC OF FREE TRADE.

An Address,

DELIVERED TO THE WEST HAM LIBERAL
ASSOCIATION, MARCH 6, 1882,

BY

EDWARD NORTH BUXTON.

CASSELL, PETTER, GALPIN & CO.:

LONDON, PARIS & NEW YORK.

1882.

THE

ABC OF FREE TRADE

An Address,

*DELIVERED TO THE WEST HAM LIBERAL
ASSOCIATION, MARCH 6, 1882,*

EDWARD NORTH BUXTON.

CASSELL, PETTER, GALPIN & CO.:
LONDON, PARIS & NEW YORK.

1882.

THE A B C OF FREE TRADE.

A HISTORIAN of our own time wrote, three or four years ago, " There is no more chance of reaction against Free Trade in England than there is of a reaction against the rule of three." This proves again the wisdom of the advice, " Don't prophesy unless you know." A party, encouraged thereto by the rash and ignorant speeches of one of its leaders, and the weak vacillation of the other, driven to straits for want of a cry, has seized upon the opportunity given by the recent depression to revive the exploded fallacies of forty years back, in the hope of winning here and there a county seat.

People are perhaps beginning to see through this move, but many even now have not had the time or inclination to familiarise themselves with the facts and the arguments which satisfied our forefathers, and it seems necessary again to furnish every elector with the reasons against a reaction which, if successful, would be full of misfortune for this country. It is not enough to be Free Traders by tradition ; we must be Free Traders by conviction, and be able to give a reason for the faith that is in us. We cannot afford to rest on our oars in the matter. The Fair Trade

League is an active and aggressive body whose conspicuous offices you may see any day in Trafalgar Square. Moreover, we cannot forget that this question was made an especial point of by our opponents in this constituency, and also in the adjoining constituency of the Tower Hamlets, at the last election; and you may still observe that the local Conservative press closely identifies itself with the Fair Trade party.

I hope no one will be offended at the title of this lecture. No doubt I shall say many things which some of you have heard before; but my object is to speak to those whose lives are so busy that they have no time to read up a subject of this kind, and trust rather to discussion, to speeches, and to lectures like this for their political opinion than to books. Before entering on argumentative matter, however, I shall ask you to compare the old Protection days, and the state of things they produced, with the state of things we live under; and I shall try to account for the reaction which has arisen in these latter days against Free Trade. I shall then seek to furnish you with a few leading principles upon which, if you once grasp them, you may rely to save you from falling into the traps of those who would lead you astray; after which I will deal with the allegations and proposals of the Fair Traders.

Now, I ask you to consider the state of things that prevailed from 1815, when the most stringent Protection Act was passed, to 1846, when Protection was finally swept away. At that time scarcely an article in general use could be imported from abroad without paying a very heavy, and in some instances an almost prohibitive, duty. The price of everything in common use was enormously enhanced; and the cost of living was immensely greater than it is now. One result of this was that people were continually trying to evade the duties by smuggling. The Custom House machinery had to be kept up at great expense, but, notwithstanding this, smuggling still went on, because nobody thought it very wrong to defraud the revenue; and many a man was first tempted into crime in this way. Joseph Hume, on one occasion, showed his silk bandana handkerchief to the House of Commons, and said, "Here is an article absolutely prohibited by your tariffs; yet most of you have one in your pocket."

Then the importation of corn was absolutely prohibited till it reached the price of 8os. a quarter. That means about 1s. 6d. per quartern loaf; and if the duty which was paid in 1840 were put on the present import of corn, it would mean an annual tax of something like £20,000,000 a year on the people's bread. The scarcity of bread caused constant riots, and the House of Commons had on several occasions to be protected by a large force.

To judge by the Poor Law returns, what is called "Protection to native industries" certainly failed to do at that time what you are told it would do now—find employment for the masses. In some towns nearly ¼th of the population were in receipt of poor relief, and everywhere great numbers were constantly out of work.

There were frequent depressions of trade of a most serious character, and, although these laws were maintained in the supposed interest of agriculture, agriculture suffered as much as any other business; and in the period of which I am speaking there were no less than five Royal Commissions to inquire into the causes of agricultural distress.

Wages were far lower than now; and certainly those who tell you that Protection would increase your wages have yet to show why it did not do so formerly.

It took a long time to eradicate the mistaken views held by many statesmen of that day. They had an idea that the one thing needful was to sell as much as possible to other nations, and to buy as little as possible from them. This is the old exploded notion of having what is called "the balance of trade" in your favour—a notion which even now lingers with some illogical people, and about which I shall have something to say presently.

The extraordinary thing is that the politicians who were in favour of Protection at that time, and, we may add, some of the present day, did not see that if Protection was a good thing for the country generally, it ought to be a good thing for a county, or even a parish. For instance, in former times a great deal of iron was made in Kent and Sussex. Now, why should they not have put a line of Custom Houses along the Thames, and imposed a heavy duty on iron coming from the north? Of course iron in those counties would be enormously dearer; but what of that? They would have "protected native industry."

, But to return to our history. The change was not a sudden one, like a transformation scene, from the evils of Protection to the blessings of Free Trade. Far-seeing men for many years had pointed out the evil of the system. Statesmen had even tinkered at it, and had tried, by sliding scales and half-measures, to mitigate the mischief. Opinion was of very slow growth, but it was sure. The agitation against the Corn Laws is an excellent lesson to those who desire to carry reforms. The leaders of the movement made but little way as long as they only tried to convert the House of Commons. When they got the ear of the constituencies they made great strides. The Anti-Corn Law League found out the secret early in the day. The laws of which we are speaking could not stand the fierce light of day which was cast upon them by the League. They first crumbled away, then cast off great masses, then came tumbling down, a complete ruin, never to be restored. But it was a long battle. The landowners fought to the death. They knew that the greater the quantity of corn, the less the price the corn-grower would get for it. Whenever an abundant harvest would have helped the people to prosperity, the monopolists cried out that they were in danger. Their interest was opposed to the interest of the people. The protected manufacturers went with them. Their principle was that if everybody paid more than was necessary for what they wanted, every one was richer all round. They played into one another's hands. They said in effect : "If you give me a little more than the market price for my corn, I can afford to pay more for your machinery and cloth." They know better now; but they were a long time learning it. But the League, or rather the truth which the League proclaimed, was too much for them, and Peel, who was appointed Minister in 1841 to uphold the Corn Laws, himself repealed them in 1846. As Mr. Bright said afterwards, " Famine itself, against which we had warred, joined us." By the time the Repeal year was reached the change could not have been long delayed, because the people had found out what they wanted. But no doubt it was a series of bad harvests and famine years that finished the business, because it set men inquiring. A

8

series of bad harvests has again in our day set men inquiring, and the result will be to confirm them in the wisdom of the decision of their fathers.

▲ And now let us turn to the bright side, and examine into the results of this great reform. Well, West Ham is one result. There is no sign so sure of continuous prosperity as a rapid increase of population, and there has been a great increase. If things had been left as they were, if we had the same restrictive laws, if we had had to feed ten millions more people on the same quantity of food, we should all have been fighting among ourselves long ago. Instead of that, other countries have poured in the tea, the sugar, and all the other commodities that we chiefly require, in such quantities, and at so cheap a rate, that every man, woman, and child was able to consume four times as much last year per head as forty years ago.

No doubt along with this prosperity there is much misery, but far less than there was in the Protection time. Notwithstanding the great increase of population, there are fewer paupers. There is far less crime. There were 34,000 convictions in 1840; in 1879 there were only 17,000. You will agree with me that saving habits in the people is a thing worth encouraging; and also that if you find people learning to save, it is a sign that they are tolerably well off. The deposits in Savings Banks have risen from £24,000,000 to nearly three times as much. If people tell you that the country is going to the bad, ask them to look at the state of the Funds, which have been higher lately than they have ever been before; so that those who deal in our National securities do not seem to have lost faith in the old country. Some people will tell you that all this is owing to steam and electricity. Steam and electricity have done much for us ; but other countries have had these advantages, and we do not find that they can show the same signs of advance as Free Trade England. People point to France and Germany; but you will find that we are ahead of them all in the progress that we have made in these forty years.

If, then, there has been this enormous expansion of prosperity, how is it that people are to be found who cry out against our system ? It is due to the prolonged and grievous depression in Trade since 1874. Let us look into this depression, and see how it arose. The Fair Traders will tell you that it is due to the heavy tariffs of other countries ; but that is at once disposed of, because the tariffs remain precisely the same as they were in 1871-2-3, the most prosperous years we ever knew. It is a curious fact that in America, where the depression prevailed to at least as great an extent, and where they live under Protection, large numbers of people began to complain of Protection and to attribute their losses to it. They are much more nearly right than our Fair Trade friends here. Now, the first reason that must occur to us all is the succession of bad harvests that we have been enduring here. The national loss has been enormous. It has been calculated at 150 millions during the past three years ; and, whatever the exact amount, this has been pure dead loss to us; and it affects not only agriculturists, but every part of the community. But there is another more potent reason than this in the feverish and unwholesome increase of trade in 1871-2-3, or rather in the reaction which followed it. We were in a very great hurry to get rich in those years. Our trade increased by leaps and bounds. It would have been much better for us if we had been content with the moderate but steady yearly increase which we had made up to that time. In that case our trade would now stand at a higher figure than it does.

The Franco-German war was partly responsible for the inflation. Those nations took large quantities of goods from us which, being too busy in killing one another, they were unable to make themselves. Then other countries were eager to borrow of us, and we were not less anxious to lend, and we did lend them vast sums. These sums went abroad, not in coin, for as a matter of fact more coin came in than went out in those years, but in goods. But at last capitalists got frightened, and ceased to lend. Trade went down, and prices dropped too, so that what trade we did was less profitable.

But if, as the Fair Traders say, this great depression, out of which we are only now beginning to emerge, is due to our Free Trade policy, how is it that Protectionist countries have suffered quite as much as we have? From 1873 to 1877 all countries were seriously depressed; and though America recovered rather more quickly than we did, that is due to the fact that, while we have had three very bad harvests, she has had exceptionally good ones, and has profited by our losses as she has had to supply our needs; but that the depression existed there, let me give one or two instances. From 1869 to 1873 the emigration to the United States was 200,000 a year. In 1874 the balance of emigration over immigration was only 1,000. In 1874 the iron industry was so depressed that nearly two-thirds of the furnaces were out of blast.

But if we really want to see how other countries are doing in comparison with our own, it is much safer to take

a somewhat longer period. Let us, for instance, compare the progress of France with our own. Our total exports were, in 1868, 225 millions ; in 1880, 286 millions. Those of France were 149 millions in 1868, and 171 millions in 1879, or hardly one-third of our progress in the same time. If we examine the imports, they tell the same tale. Now look at Protectionist Germany. Well, I will not trouble you with figures which you may find it hard to remember; I will simply read you what the German Chambers of Commerce say of their present system :—
"Perhaps no critic of the new system was prepared for the rapidity of the decision with which the consequences of the Protective tariff have shown themselves : first, in increasing the difficulties of trade ; secondly, in raising the prices of the necessaries of life ; thirdly, in injuring the prosperity of the labouring classes."

America, owing to her boundless resources, to the limitless extent of new land ready to be occupied almost for the asking, to the streams of able-bodied labourers who are poured into her borders from this side of the Atlantic, to her lack of a standing army, to her varied mineral wealth, and the genius of her people, cannot but make great strides. But it is in spite of Protection, not in consequence of it. Then you must always remember that she enjoys absolute Free Trade throughout her vast dominions, and that is as if all the countries of Europe enjoyed Free Trade among themselves. Nevertheless, her Protection policy has almost killed her foreign trade—always excepting the enormous quantity of corn and grain of all kinds as well as cotton which, thanks to our open ports, she sends to us, and which has so largely tended to the well-

being of our people. While we export 180 millions of manufactured articles, America only exports 15 millions.

So far we have seen that during the Protectionist
period England was far poorer and suffered far more from
depressed trade than she has ever done since. After
changing her policy she has advanced greatly in wealth
and prosperity; and though there have been seasons of
depression, each wave of good times has mounted higher
than the last. The progress has been continuous. We
have also seen that while other nations have made progress,
they have not done so in the same proportion as we have,
or so rapidly as they would have done under wiser
fiscal laws.

Before proceeding to discuss the allegations of the
Fair Traders, I want you to take in one or two simple propositions which must be grasped before the rights of the
question are understood. Without them you are lost; but
these once mastered, you can defy and demolish all the Fair
Traders in the kingdom. No doubt these propositions are
familiar to nine-tenths of you, but I do not apologise for
repeating them, because I am here to-night, not to convince
those who are already convinced, but to confirm those who
are doubting.

The first proposition is that all goods bought from other
countries are paid for, not with gold, but by other goods
which are sent back to them.

The second is that duties on goods are paid for by the
people who consume those goods, and not by the people
who produce them—by the importing, not by the exporting
country.

The first proposition is easily proved. The fallacy we

have got to get rid of is this—that all commodities are paid for in gold, and if you can only get in more gold than you pay out you must get richer. But the truth is, that the goods we buy from other countries are paid for, not in gold, but in goods that we send to those countries. An account is kept of all the bullion that passes from one country to another, which, as a matter of fact, is, quite insignificant in amount. In the case of the enormous indemnity which France paid to Germany, hardly any specie was transferred. Again, in the years 1871, 1872, and 1873 we lent to other countries about 400 millions, but during that period not only did no gold leave the country, but the balance was slightly the other way; and if you think a moment this result must always ensue. We keep just as much of the precious metals as we require for currency and for ornamental purposes, and no more. A very small withdrawal of gold from the currency of the country raises the rate of interest, and this at once tempts back what has gone out.

It follows that the export of goods is paid for by the import of goods. If it were not so, consider what would happen. Suppose we were able to export largely and import nothing, and were to be paid in gold. There would presently be too much gold—more than we wanted—and the only effect of that would be that everything would be dearer. The baker would get more for his bread, but he would have to pay more for his meat; and so on all round, so that no one would be a bit the richer. Everything would be so much dearer here that the foreigner would cease to buy from us, and we should lose our export trade as well as our import, and that is all we should get by our move, supposing it to be possible. Thus, goods that you buy *must* be paid for by goods that you sell, and if you limit your imports by imposing duties, you limit your exports as well. All trade is barter. If you sell your goods, and with the money buy other goods, you in effect exchange your own goods for those you want.

No doubt some one may say, "How is it then that some nations import much more than they export, and that the contrary is the case elsewhere?" The answer is that if a country exports more than it imports it is because it has previously borrowed from other countries, and has to repay the debt, or the interest on the debt, in goods. In the same way, if a country imports more than it exports, like England, it is because other countries stand indebted to it. If it were the case that the difference is paid for in gold, we in England should have to pay out more than 100 millions a year, and we should very soon get to the end of every scrap we have got either in circulation or in use ; so that you could not do it even if you sacrificed every sovereign and wedding-ring and silver thimble in existence. Now I hope you know, if you did not know before, that goods are paid for, not with gold, but with other goods.

The second fallacy that we have got to get rid of is this—that if we impose duties on any article from abroad, the people who send us the article will pay the duty and not we. One would think that we need only appeal to the universal experience of commercial men to refute this. It is always the case that if a country imposes a duty, the price of the article on which the duty is imposed is enhanced. But let us prove it by taking a simple case. Supposing there is some article which is produced here and sells in our markets for £20 a ton. It is made at a fair profit, because competition between manufacturers prevents any one making an excessive profit. Now suppose that some other country imports from us some of that article, and puts on a duty of £5 a ton. Do you suppose that that article will still sell in the other country for £20? Certainly not. The duty will be added to the cost there, because competition is such that the manufacturer here already takes as little as he can afford, and if he took less he would make no profit but a loss. I find in this morning's paper the following paragraph :—"A new trade has sprung up between Scotland and America—that of " Champion " potatoes. These are shipped at Aberdeen at 36s. a ton. They are subject to a duty of £1 per ton, and are expected to realise £4 to £4 10s. in New York." But if the Fair Traders are right, this last anticipation would not be fulfilled. According to them, the shipper on this side would, in some mysterious way, have to pay the £1 duty out of his 36s. If that be so, the " Champions " would be amazingly cheap. If that instance does not satisfy you, what do you say to those articles of which there are some exported from this country to America which have to pay a duty there of 100 per cent. ? In that case the merchants on this side of the water must absolutely give away the goods, according to the theory of the Fair Traders. John Bull, we know, is a long-suffering and generous person, but he is not quite so meek as that.

Now I hope you have taken hold of those two prime articles of faith. Armed with them, let us go forth and do battle with the revived Protectionists. Let us examine fairly, without prejudice, the allegations which are brought out after forty years, and rubbed up to look new.

First and foremost, it is said: that our imports
largely exceed our exports—which is quite true. But it is
not true to go on and say that we are therefore
wasting our substance, and living on our capital, like a
spendthrift who is spending more than he gets in. In the
first place, it is a great mistake to suppose that all this heap
of imports is spent and consumed and wasted. On the
contrary, it represents, as Dr. Johnson said, a "boundless
potentiality of wealth." A very large part of it is raw
material, which is worked up here into manufactured articles,
and goes abroad again at a vastly increased value. Cotton,
for instance, comes here in the rough and leaves us again, at
weight for weight, hundreds of times the value; and in the
meanwhile our workmen, who are creating the wealth, are
fed and clothed out of these imports which frighten some
people so much.

People who tell you that we are buying more than we sell,
and therefore must be getting poorer, evidently have got
hold of the notion, which I have already shown you to be a
mistaken one, that commodities are paid for in gold. They
fancy that because we import goods to the value of
100 millions a year more than we export, this 100 millions
leaves the country in the shape of gold; but so far from this
being the case, on an average of years rather more bullion
comes into the country than goes out of it. Let us then
examine why it is that we get into the country so much
more of goods than we send out, and whether this is a sign
of impoverishment or wealth. Upon this hinges the whole
question between us and the Fair Traders, and if you
master this you have mastered the most difficult part of the
problem. The Fair Traders say that we buy of the foreigner

411 million pounds' worth of goods, and sell him only 286 millions' worth, and the balance of 125 millions is so much loss to us and gain to the foreigner. The Free Trader, on the other hand, says it is not a question of buying and selling at all, but of exchange ; and if we get in four or five pounds' worth for every three we send out, that shows we are doing a profitable business. And it is this question of profit which accounts for a large part of the excess of imports. If a merchant sent abroad goods worth a given sum to him, and got back in exchange goods worth only the same amount, it is clear that he would have made, not only no profit, but a dead loss, because he would have had to pay for freight and insurance. Take an instance close at home. Corn-dealers sometimes do a little trade in artificial manures. Suppose a corn-dealer at Romford to purchase 20 quarters of wheat at home for £50. He sends it to London, and sells it for £55. With the money he purchases artificial manure, which he brings home and sells for £60 in Romford. His import into Romford would exceed his export by £10, and yet it would not be an unprofitable transaction. It would be very unprofitable ‑ indeed if his imports only balanced his exports. But now suppose he employs a fellow-townsman to do his carting for him at so much a load. Whatever this might amount to, by so much would the town of Romford be the richer. And this brings me to the second item which accounts for the difference between exports and imports—that of Freight and Insurance. Owing to the great advantage which Free Trade gives us, of the total ocean-carried trade of the world about one-half is carried in British ships. It has been calculated that about 60 millions

a year is earned in this way by England. This is not included in the exports, but is included in the imports. So here we have another heavy item to account for the difference of the two, and the whole of it goes to add to the wealth of the country. But then there is another item more important still, which represents the indebtedness of other nations to us. It is calculated that about 50 millions a year are paid to us for interest—not in cash, but in goods. And even if we could suddenly stop all exports to other countries, this debt must be discharged to us, and must be sent to us in the form of goods. Here we have, then, three items quite big enough to account for the difference between our exports and imports.

Now let us look at it from another point of view. If the contention of the Fair Traders, that we are living on our capital, and that this excess of imports means wasting our substance, is true, how is it that we have not long ago been ruined? If you take the last forty years, you will find that this excess of imports amounts to no less a sum than 1,600 millions. If it is true that this is so much loss to the country, we must long ago have been bankrupt. This fact alone is enough to refute and reduce to an absurdity the notion that these balances are paid for in gold; but, as a matter of fact, during these forty years we have imported rather more specie than we sent out—a sum amounting on an average to about one million a year. Does any one suppose that we owe this enormous amount to foreign nations? On the contrary, during these forty years we have increased our investments abroad by about 1,000 millions. So far, then, is it from being true that we are growing poorer, owing to the excess of imports over exports, it is demonstrable that we have grown enormously richer while it has been going on. And the great increase of our investments abroad has not been made by drawing upon our wealth at home. On the contrary, while it has been going on, our wealth has been largely increasing. If you doubt this, look at the Income Tax returns.

And now, if you want further confirmation of what I have stated, that the excess of imports is to a large extent due to accumulated wealth, look at other nations whose position is the reverse of ours, and who export more than they import, and you will invariably find that it is the nations who have been heavy borrowers in the past who are in this position.

There is one very instructive instance of a country which for a time exported more than it imported, and has since reversed the process. That country is France, and the period when its exports were in excess—a state of things that the Fair Traders tell you is a sign of such prosperity—was in the four years immediately following the Franco-German war, and it was caused by the enormous indemnity which France had to pay out to Germany. Thus, as Mr. Chamberlain remarked the other day, if our Fair Trade friends want to stop our excess of imports, all they have got to do is to engage in a good long European war, and to do that they must first of all bring the late Government back into power. Then they must take care to get well beaten, and saddled with the payment of 200 or 300 millions indemnity, and you will have the result at once.

Another contention of the Fair Traders is that to put duties on our imports would be to multiply industries at home, and increase the rate of wages. The direct contrary

is the fact; and if it were not so, how is it that wages are at
least 50 per cent. higher than they were forty years ago?
It is perfectly true that wages in Protectionist America are
higher than they are here, but then it is also true that ·
wages in Protectionist France are lower than they are here;
and it is a curious fact that while our opponents sometimes
appeal to America as showing what Protection does for
wages, they not less frequently appeal to the low wages in
France, and call out for Protection against the competition
which is caused by the low wages and long hours of labour
in that country. They cannot use both arguments; one
must be wrong. The fact is, that the rate of wages is
chiefly governed by supply and demand, and in a new
country, where labour is scarce and commerce active,
whether it is Free Trade or Protectionist, wages will rule
high. At the same time, other things being equal, wages
will rule higher in a Free Trade country than in a Protected
one, because Free Trade promotes commerce, and commerce creates a demand for labour which raises the price.
But then, our opponents say, Protection fosters fresh industries which would not otherwise have existed, and therefore
improves trade. It may foster fresh industries; but if it
does, it is at the expense of other industries which need no
fostering. What it does is not to create additional work,
but to divert capital from work that is naturally profitable
to work that is not profitable, and which can only be made
so by artificial means. What we should aim at is division
of labour—to sell as much as we possibly can of the things
which we can make cheapest and best, and that will
enable us to buy the equivalent of things which the foreigner
can make cheapest and best. If we take the opposite

advice, and foster protected industries, it is as if a skilled artisan, earning high wages, were to say to himself, "Why should I buy all the goods I want for the use of my family? Why should I not grind my own corn, and bake it; and make my own boots and coats, and my wife's dresses?" The effect of such a policy would be to divert the greater part of his time from what paid him well to what paid him badly, and his commodities would be badly made into the bargain. This would be "protecting native industry" with a vengeance; but though it may be thought an extreme case, it is a fair illustration of what happens when the same thing is done on a large scale.

But to return to the question of wages. I do not for a moment contend that there has not been in some cases a heavy fall in wages during the depression in trade which we have experienced. What I say is, that this is due to temporary causes, and in no way to Free Trade. On the contrary, Free Trade has enabled us to bear the fall in a way which would not have been the case if it had not been for the access which it gave us to cheap food. Even during the depressed period pauperism has steadily diminished, emigration has steadily diminished, crime has steadily diminished, and the Excise returns have steadily increased. The fact is, the well-being of the people depends, not only on the absolute amount of the wages they earn, but also on the purchasing power of those wages. Almost every important article used by working-men is cheaper than it used to be, and more of it is consequently used by them. Thus, the consumption of sugar is one-half as much again per head as it was twelve years ago; and if you go further back, the difference is still more marked, being now four times as great as it was in 1840. You will find the consumption of tea to have increased in much the same proportion.

This complaint about the fall of wages being due to Free Trade does not come from working-men. Though here and there there have been murmurs, it has generally been found that they were bogus working-men who have uttered them—put forward by others for their own ulterior purposes. The Trades' Union Congress, which may be taken much more nearly to represent the opinion of the working classes, emphatically and indignantly repudiated these pernicious doctrines.

Another allegation of the Fair Traders is that we have been driven out of the neutral markets of the world. It is, no doubt, perfectly true that as to six countries of the world our trade has been reduced. The six are—America, Germany, Russia, Holland, Egypt, and the South American republics. In the case of the first four, this is primarily due to their increased import duties. In the case of Egypt and South America, it is due to the fact that for a considerable period we lent these countries large sums of money. Those loans went to them, of course, in the form of goods, but we have found that our debts are not likely to be repaid in that or any other form; and as the burnt child dreads the fire, so we have ceased to lend them any more. That is why our exports to these two countries have diminished. But even including these six countries where our trade has diminished, and taking the year 1879, which was the worst of the depressed years, our total trade far exceeded that of any other nation. It was 611 millions in that year. That was our total trade, with our 35 millions of population. Germany, with 40 millions of people, did 370 millions of trade; the United States, with 50 millions of people, did only 238 millions; and. so on. So that you see we can afford to lump these two great Protectionist countries together, and still beat them in the gross amount of trade we do, and, man for man, do three times as much. If you look at our exports alone they tell the same story. In spite of Protection we send to nearly every country in the world more goods than any other nation does. So that the allegation that we are beaten is not even true in protected countries, still less is it true in neutral markets. Wherever we meet other sellers on fair and equal terms, there is no comparison at all between us; we are far away ahead. Throughout the continents of Asia, Africa, and Australia, other countries cannot hold a candle to us. For instance, over that great area the trade of the United States amounts to £4,751,000, while ours reaches 78 millions. The iron trade is frequently cited as one in which we are being overhauled by Belgium, but the exports of Belgium in this staple are less than one-tenth of ours.

If it were true that other countries could beat us in neutral markets, they could also beat us here at home. But that certainly is not the case. We import hardly any manufactures from other countries, and when people tell you our home market is flooded with foreign manufacture it is simply untrue.. What we do import is chiefly food, and the raw material which we work up into finished manufactures and sell again at a great profit. Nine-tenths of our imports consist of these, and only one-tenth of manufactures; but when you look at what we send abroad, you find that 92 per cent. of that consists of manufactured articles. And these won-

derful results are no miracle ; they are the direct consequence
of the fact that all commodities are cheaper here than they
are elsewhere. Our workers carry on the competition on
the best possible conditions. They are fed, and clothed,
and housed at the lowest rate, and far better than elsewhere.
Thus they can produce more cheaply, and they can afford
to undersell the Protectionists even in Protectionist countries—very often with goods which are taxed to the extent of
50 or 100 per cent.

I do not think I need dwell very long, after what I have
already said, on the next allegation of the new school of Protectionists, that "one-sided Free Trade is bad for this country."
A more straightforward way of putting the complaint would be
to say, "'No bread' is better than 'half a loaf.'" It is founded
on the fallacy that we buy what we want as a favour to
other countries ; whereas the truth is we buy these things
because we want them, and because we must, from the nature
of things, receive them in payment for the huge total of goods
which we send abroad, for the ocean-carrying which we do
for other nations as well as ourselves, and, lastly, in payment
of interest on the enormous debt which other countries have
contracted to this country.

I now come to the remedy which is proposed by the Fair
Traders for the state of things of which they complain. They
suggest Reciprocity, or rather Retaliation, on the foreigner.
We are to put duties on the goods we import from them, in
the hope that they will take off the duties they impose on
ours ; that is to say, we are to injure ourselves at the same
time that we injure them, in the hope that they will abandon
their policy, which we know injures both them and us. We are
to become Protectionists in the hope of persuading them to

become Free Traders. We might just as well say to the Jews, "Unless you become Christians we will adopt your faith and become Jews;" or to the Conservatives, "Unless you become Liberals we will adopt your principles and become Tories." Would not foreigners at once say, "You seem to have very little faith in your own principles. Either Free Trade is a good thing or a bad thing. If it is good, why do you abandon it? If it is bad, why do you ask us to adopt it?" We hope that some day other countries will see that their Protectionist policy is good neither for themselves nor us, but such an argument as that would certainly retard the change. The course they would probably take would be to retaliate still further upon us; and here we encounter the chief difficulty in the way of Retaliation. Foreigners could retaliate with far more effect against us than we can against them, because our imports of their manufactures are far less than their imports of ours. I will go into that matter presently, but in the meanwhile I want you to consider what the effect would be upon ourselves. Whether other countries increase their duties against us or not, there is no doubt about the effect which taxing our imports would have on our own trade. It would at once diminish those imports, and it follows that our exports would diminish also, because they pay for one another. If we limit our purchases from other countries, we also limit their power of purchasing from us. The country would be impoverished by the reduction of our foreign trade; and at the same time the prices of commodities would be raised at home.

Well, then, I want to know whether we are to levy these duties against all other countries alike, or are we to single out particular countries, and tax their commodities only?

If we are going to treat all alike, that will be making no distinction between those who treat us well and those who treat us badly; so that is out of the question. If, on the other hand, you are going to pick out the countries that tax our goods, there is this practical difficulty. What security have you that the country against which you raise the barrier would not evade it by sending their goods through another country against which it does not exist? For instance, if we put a duty on French silks, what is to prevent their being sent here through Belgium?

Then, again, these measures of Retaliation—are they to be permanent or temporary? If they do not have the desired effect of coercing other countries—which they certainly would not—are we to advance further on the downward path, or to recede? If we were to enter on that path, we should probably be unable to help going further, because those who did not happen to be interested in the particular articles protected would soon get tired of paying higher for them, and would call out for Protection for the articles they themselves produce. But supposing, as the more reasonable Fair Traders would no doubt say, it is intended to be a temporary measure, you would for a few years have diverted capital into trades which could not stand alone, and then, having fostered them in this way, have left them in the lurch. The effect of that would be ruin and disaster to those whom you had tempted out of other branches of trade, where they needed no such bolstering.

But now comes the question, upon what imports do you propose to put a duty? Is it to be upon raw materials, or manufactured articles, or food? We may leave raw materials out of the question. No one seriously proposes it. The Fair Trade agitation proceeds chiefly from a few manufacturers, and they know too much to propose that the raw material which they purchase should be raised in price. There remain, then, duties on manufactures and on food. Which is it to be? Judging by recent experience in by-elections, it is to be one thing in one place and another thing in another. The Conservative candidate who stands for a county goes in boldly for a duty on corn, to please the agriculturists; but this would never do in the towns, where people eat bread but do not grow it; so another Conservative candidate in that case tries to please the manufacturers. But the Fair Trade League consists of both these classes, and it has therefore to adopt a policy combining both programmes. No doubt what the manufacturers would like best would be duties on manufactured goods; but they see the hopelessness of proposing this without allies, so they hold out a tempting bait to the agriculturists to join them, and go in with a light heart for a duty on corn as well. Let me read you what they recommend :—

" A very moderate duty to be levied on all articles of food from foreign countries, the same being admitted free from all parts of our own empire prepared to take our manufactures in reasonably free exchange ; " and then, again, " adequate import duties " on foreign manufactures.

Let us, then, examine what the effect of these two proposals would be. A duty on manufactures is a very dangerous weapon for us to use, and more likely to explode backwards than forwards, for our manufactures are that part of our trade in which we are most vulnerable. Our imports of manufactures are 45 millions, but our exports are nearly 200 millions; so you see that if we once begin the game of

Retaliation there is no doubt which side can hit hardest. If I were to fight a duel with the smallest man in the room, it is clear that he would have a great advantage over me, because he would have so much more to shoot at. In the same way we are open to attack all over the 200 millions, and can only impose duties on 45 millions, and, indeed, in practice that total would have to be largely reduced, as it includes many items which practically could not be taxed, because, though nominally manufactures, they must be regarded as raw materials, as they are further worked up here. Take a particular case—that of America, which is certainly the greatest sinner, and therefore the nation whom the Fair Traders are most anxious to attack. We send to America twenty-four millions of manufactures, but we take from her only a little over four millions. With what prospect of success should we go to them and say, " We will tax your four millions unless you untax our twenty-four millions." They would say, " Do so, if you like ; it will have the smallest possible effect on us. We shall be happy to put on another 10 per cent. on your twenty-four millions." In such a war of tariffs as that we should be fighting against enormous odds, and should inevitably be worsted.

True, it is sometimes said, "But why not put a tax on luxuries?" only the worst of it is the doctors differ as to what are luxuries. For instance, Sir John Holker, speaking at Preston, defined luxuries upon which he would put duties as "beef, mutton, and the crops." I don't know whether he would go so far as to say that, being luxuries, working-men could very well do without them. But we may fairly suppose that silk and wine are the luxuries intended. There is, of course, far less objection to this than to some of the other proposals, and, as a brewer, I ought rather to encourage the tax on light wine being increased ; but there is this objection even to this proposal. For every pound's worth of silk and wine that we import we must export somewhere a corresponding value of goods ; and if you limit our import you limit our export as well. Our total of trade is thereby diminished, and some one here in England earns less. No doubt, now our treaty with France is about to expire, there will be an outcry for duties on those articles, and it would be entirely within our right to impose them ; but, in my opinion, it would be a mistake to do so. I believe a better way to bring the French to their senses would be, instead of increasing the duties on French wines, to reduce those on Spanish wines.

The alternative proposal is for a 5s. duty on corn, and some people even go so far as to assert that such a duty would be paid, not by the people who buy the corn, but by those who sell it to us on the other side of the Atlantic. That is to say, that if we put on a 5s. duty, corn will not be any dearer here, but growers will accept 5s. a quarter less in America. But if that were possible, they would prefer to sell it at the market price at home. It is not to be supposed that growers who send their corn here would continue to do so for benevolent motives when they could get 5s. a quarter more by selling it for home consumption. But perhaps it will be even asserted that the effect would be to cheapen all corn in the United States by 5s., whether consumed there or exported. How very grateful the Americans would be to us ! But not for long. Every grower of corn cultivates that crop because it pays him better than any other. To some, no doubt, it pays much better ; to others the difference is slight—1s., 2s., 3s., as the case may be.   To knock down the price 5s. would thus at once destroy the profit of growing corn over a large area.   If this impossible reduction in price were effected, other crops would be substituted, or, in the case of the distant West, where the farmers are handicapped by long railway carriage, land might go out of cultivation.   The supply of corn would be diminished, and the price would rise at least to its former level in America ; and as the duty must be paid by some one, it must come out of the consumers' pockets.

Then, again, there is a suggestion that we should, while putting this duty on American-grown corn, accept it free from our North American colonies.   But if Canada cannot at present compete with the United States in the price they can afford to take for their corn, it is because it costs them more to grow it and transport it ; so in this case again we should have to pay the higher price.   Then, what is to prevent the Americans sending their corn through Canada, and so avoiding the 5s. duty ?   The Canadians, it is true, might also impose the duty of 5s., as against their neighbours, but would they be prepared to bear the enormous cost of Custom Houses to prevent smuggling over the thousands of miles of land frontier ?   Besides, it is assumed that we are to make these concessions to Canada in return for free access to her ports ; but is there any reason to think that the Canadians would be more willing to grant them than the Americans are ?

But do the Fair Trade League really think that duties would not have the effect of increasing the price ?   If they are of this opinion, why do they object to taxing raw materials? If it is true that the exporters pay the duty in one case, it must be true in the other. Then, again, what do the League mean by such a remark as this: "They would do equal justice to the classes interested in agriculture, who are entitled to the same treatment as those connected with manufactures"? If, as they say, there would be no enhancement of price, where is the " equal justice" to the agriculturist?

To most people, at any rate, it is clearer than day that if you impose the duty at all it will have the effect of enhancing the price of bread here; and, once convinced of that fact, no patriotic Englishman would propose it. Of course, I should not for a moment accuse the Fair Traders of want of patriotism, only that they are so mentally colour-blind that they fail to see what is obvious to ninety-nine out of every hundred who have thought out the question.

Now, I have tried to compress into an hour the leading arguments of the case against a rash meddling with the freedom of importation which we enjoy. If I had the time, which that clock reminds me I have not, and if I had the gift for it, which I have not, I would sum up what I have said in an eloquent peroration; but I feel, from the attention with which you have listened to me, that your judgment is with me on this matter, and that stronger than any words of mine will be your determination that the comfort of your homes, and the well-being of all Englishmen, shall not be lightly sacrificed to the exigencies of party strife.

www.ingramcontent.com/pod-product-compliance
Lightning Source LLC
Chambersburg PA
CBHW021551270326
41930CB00008B/1457